Epidemics of Christianity

Epidemics of Christianity

A Devotional Study Guide

Dr. John Thomas Clark, ThM, DMin

Tetelestai Press

Epidemics of Christianity: A Devotional Study Guide

© 2020 Copyright by Dr. John Thomas Clark

Published by Tetelestai Press

ISBN: 978-1-7353359-2-6

EPIDEMICS DEVOTIONAL STUDY[1]

An epidemic is the rapid spread of disease to a large number of people within a given population in a short period of time. Once introduced into a population, infectious micro-organisms can spread from person to person, and, if one person transfers the infection to another person, the number of cases can grow exponentially. The worldwide Coronavirus (COVID-19) pandemic is the most recent of many epidemics that have struck mankind throughout its history.

Unfortunately, what is true of infectious diseases is also true of "wrong thinking" in the Christian life. Wrong thinking is spreading like an epidemic in Christianity, and it is causing great damage to the Church of Jesus Christ. The Epidemics of Christianity that will be discussed in this study are the following:

What Is Jesus Up To?

Introduction: If you could know exactly what Jesus Christ is interested in and passionate about and, if you could know exactly how Jesus Christ would spend His time if He was on earth today, would you want to know? Thankfully, the Word of God tells us that the primary thing Jesus Christ is passionate about is **BUILDING** His Church! However, many distractions have crept in and infiltrated our churches, much like epidemic diseases – these must be recognized and rejected (true social distancing).

Years ago, a church in California went into its surrounding neighborhoods and took a survey about what kind of church people would like to attend. After gathering the results, the members went on to create a church based upon the surveys.[1] Now, is that how we should do church?

People have so many different opinions on what church ***should be***…in fact, if you took 200 surveys, you would probably have 400 opinions. ***BUT***, whose view of church actually matters? – Not yours, not mine, but Jesus Christ's. Many of us are guilty of taking one aspect of truth (as it relates to the church) and elevating it above other similarly weighted aspects of truth. Some examples of that are the following:

1. People are the church; therefore, I can have church any time there are other Christians around, including my immediate family, and thus I don't have to go to a building to do church.

2. I am all about getting equipped, but I get my equipping online via the internet, and thus I do not need to belong to a local assembly.

3. I go to a parachurch Bible study, and thus I do not have to go to a local church on Sunday.

Now, technically, there is some truth embedded in these statements. However, notice the mindset communicated: "I don't **HAVE TO**" and basically "You **CAN'T MAKE ME!**" Ultimately, the point is NOT whether or not you **HAVE TO** do something - it is what the Lord Jesus desires for you and His local church. Some questions for people who might take issue with this, include the following:

1. How can you have elders or deacons, as instituted to consider the leaders of the church of Jesus Christ if you are meeting solely with your family at home?

2. How can the elders "shepherd" you if they do not even know you because you are piping into their online services from home?

3. How can you "rub shoulders" with other believers and spur them on to love and to good deeds if you never have face-to-face interactions with other believers?

4. What would happen in a parachurch Bible study if someone

started to promote and teach false doctrine? What biblical warrant or authority would one have to put that person out of the group?

Thoughtful quote: We live in a self-centered, consumer-oriented world that looks at life, religion included, primarily from a selfish point of view. And this world viewpoint all too easily rubs off on Christians. A large portion of the Christian community sees the blessings and provisions God has given us in Christ as designed strictly for our own personal happiness and comfort. Our tendency today is to make satisfaction and personal comfort our religion…most Christian "how-to" books regularly explore our needs in a self-absorbed way that treats our enjoyment of life rather than the glory of God as the center of interest.[2]

Read Matthew 16:13-18. The first mention of the word "Church" in the Bible is found in Matthew 16:18, and it follows the conversation Jesus had with His disciples starting in Matthew 16:13.

Jesus' statement in Matthew 16:18 about building His church was made following Israel's national rejection of Jesus by its leaders in Matthew 12:22-45. At this point, Christ's focus began to shift from offering the Kingdom to Israel to foretelling His coming death and resurrection (Matthew 12:38-40) and the building of His Church. Jesus' mention of the Church here came from a conversation between Him and His disciples that began in Matthew 16:13 where Jesus asked them a simple question: *"Who do people say that the Son of Man is?"* When the disciples said that people speculated He was John the Baptist, Elijah, Jeremiah, or even one of the prophets, Jesus asked them directly, *"But who do you say that I am?"* in Matthew 16:15. Simon Peter's rock-solid declaration in Matthew 16:16, *"You are the Christ, the Son of the living God,"* was what Jesus referred to in Matthew 16:18 when He said, *"Upon this rock I will build My church."*

Questions for further study:

1. In verse 18, Jesus says, "Upon this rock I will build my church." What rock was He talking about?

     a. Why would the correct identity of this **ROCK** be important? See also Matthew 21:42, Acts 4:11, Romans 9:33, 1 Corinthians 3:11, Ephesians 2:20, and 1 Peter 2:4, 6-7.

2. Based upon verse 18, WHO is the one building the Church, and whose Church is it?

     a. In terms of understanding Jesus' passion, priorities, and interests at this time in history, why is it important to know WHO is building the Church?

     b. Do you think Jesus is committed to finishing the job of building the Church? How does He intend to accomplish this task? Can you think of any verses to support your answer?

3. Building projects do not typically happen overnight, so WHAT does the word "build" imply about this Church-building project, and WHO does Jesus intend to include in this project? See 1 Corinthians 3:5-9 and Ephesians 4:11-16.

4. Jesus' building project is proactive as shown by the phrase: "The gates of hades will not overpower it." Typically, gates keep people out, so when Jesus says this, what is He referring to?

Epidemic #1: Poor Conflict Resolution

Introduction: In this section, we are going to look at one of the epidemics that is spreading and doing great harm to the Church of today – poor conflict resolution. Many Christians desire "church" to be free of any conflicts or drama because their lives are filled with both these things in every other sphere (family, friendships, work, etc.). Unfortunately, for those wanting to avoid conflict, conflict is a tool in God's toolbelt designed for one's spiritual growth and for the health of His Church. If this is the case, how can we engage in conflict well?

In order to further introduce the topic of conflict resolution, a funny story is in order. Once there was a man shipwrecked on a deserted island. He was an industrious, hard-working man, so, by the time he was rescued fifteen years later, he had managed to transform the island into a collection of roads and buildings. The people who rescued him were amazed at his accomplishments and asked for a tour of the island. He was more than happy to oblige. "The first building on our left," he began, "is my house. You'll see that I have a comfortable three-bedroom estate, complete with indoor plumbing and a sprinkler system. There is also a storage shed in the back for all my lawn tools." The rescue party was astonished. It was better than some of their homes on the mainland. "That building over there is the store where I do my grocery shopping. Next to it is my bank and across the street is the gym where I exercise." The rescuers noticed two other buildings and asked what they were. "The one on the left is where I go to church." "And the one on the right?" they inquired. "Oh, that's where I *used* to go to church."[1]

A great working definition of "conflict," taken from Ken Sande's book "The Peace Maker," is a difference in opinion or purpose that frustrates someone's goals or desires.[2] Many people believe that conflict in general is bad and is to be avoided at all cost. Many believers even believe that the early churches, as recorded in Acts, were the ideal churches, free from conflict and in perfect unity. However, contrary to public opinion, the first century churches were filled with conflict. Consider the following non-exhaustive list:

1. Church of Antioch (Acts 15:36-41) – Paul and Barnabas had conflict which resulted in separation - ministry disagreement.

2. Church of Jerusalem & Judea/Churches of Galatia (Acts 15:1-34, Galatians) – Conflict over whether or not circumcision was required to be saved – doctrinal disagreement.

3. Church of Rome (Romans 14 & 15) – Conflict over non-essential things such as food, days, or observances – practical application disagreement.

4. Church of Rome (Romans 16:17-18) – Conflict with brethren who

cause divisions and offenses contrary to sound doctrine – doctrinal disagreement.

5. Church of Corinth (1 Corinthians 1:10-13; 3:4-6) – Conflict with brethren and divisions over who they were following – ministry disagreement.

6. Church of Corinth (1 Corinthians 5:1-13) – Conflict with how to deal with a brother living in defiant and open sin – ministry disagreement.

7. Church of Corinth (1 Corinthians 6:1-8) – Conflict with brethren and attempting to solve conflicts via the secular court system – practical application disagreement.

8. Church of Corinth (1 Corinthians 12-14) – Conflict in the use and abuse of spiritual gifts – practical application disagreement.

9. Church of Corinth (1 Corinthians 15) – Conflict over the resurrection and its implications – doctrinal disagreement.

10. Church of Corinth (2 Corinthians 7:2-12) – Conflict between Paul and the Corinthian church due to his correction of them and their response to his correction – ministry and practical application disagreement.

11. Church of Ephesus/Church of Colossae (Ephesians 5-6 & Colossians 3-4) – Conflict between husbands and wives, parents and children, and employers and employees – practical application disagreement.

12. Church of Ephesus (1 Timothy 6:1-5) – Conflict between Timothy and false teachers regarding sound doctrine – doctrinal disagreement.

13. Church of Ephesus (3 John 9-10) – Conflict between John and Diotrephes who was maliciously slandering John and also disfellowshipping people when they showed hospitality to those whom he had personally written off – ministry and practical application disagreement.

14. Church of Philippi (Philippians 4:2-3) – Conflict between two women in the church – personality disagreement or practical application disagreement.

15. Church of Thessalonica (2 Thessalonians 3:6-12) – Conflict between believers in the church regarding disorderly and disruptive behavior (including laziness and not being willing to work) – doctrinal and practical application disagreement.

16. Churches of Crete (Titus 3:9-11) – Conflict between believers and divisive men who distract with unprofitable disputes – doctrinal and practical application disagreement.

17. YOUR CURRENT LOCAL CHURCH! Consider the following questions and answer honestly:

    a. Have you ever been around someone whose personality grated on yours? You know that you are supposed to love them, but you do not even like them!

b. Have you ever done ministry with someone who wants to do things a different way than you do? If they do it different than you, it means the "wrong" way, right? :-)

c. Have you ever had someone correct you and the way you parent your children? Or, even worse, have you ever had someone correct your child directly?

d. Does it bother you and grate on your nerves when someone in the church says he or she will do something, and he or she consistently does not keep their commitments?

e. Have you ever been frustrated with someone who avoids conflict at any cost, even when they are asked outright about what is bothering them, AND they deny that anything is bothering them?

Thoughtful quote: Is conflict good or bad? Consider the following quote taken from Jean Varnier, founder of L'Arche communities, "Communities need tensions if they are to grow and deepen. Tensions come from conflicts..."[3]

The Good, The Bad, and The Ugly of Conflict:

Conflict is **GOOD** because:

1. God uses it to develop our character. One does not need patience, forbearance, longsuffering, gentleness, love, and

kindness when everyone else sees things his or her way. Because of the need that conflict produces, in order to deal with conflict in a biblical way, we ***must*** be walking by means of the Spirit! Alexander Strauch in his book "If You Bite & Devour One Another," stated: "Conflict presents one of the toughest challenges to walking by the Spirit. If only we would recognize that every conflict is a test as to whether or not we will display Christlike character, the wisdom from above, and the reality of the gospel in our lives."[4]

2. God uses it to produce healthy relationships. Author Larry Crabb writes, "The difference between spiritual and unspiritual community is not whether conflict exists but is rather in our attitude toward it and our approach to handling it."[5]

3. God uses it to build His Church! (See Galatians 2:11-16)

Conflict is **BAD** because of two main responses:

1. We do not respond well to conflict, and thus we set the stage for avoiding conflict in the future. In fact, many people respond with a variety of defensive and even combative responses to conflict: anger, verbal assault, physical assault, etc. Their approach to conflict is to win at all costs!

OR

2. We avoid conflict outright. We live in a day and age where the prevalent way of dealing with conflict is to put our heads in the sand. It seems that many people are too lazy to engage in the hard, time consuming, and emotionally draining aspects of conflict resolution. For some it is just **too** hard! Now, some may seek to overlook an offense (which is biblical at times), but the problem is that our feelings do not often overlook offenses. We dwell on them or let them grow into pent-up bitterness or anger. Often things under pressure explode - including Christians.

Both of these responses have one thing in common...they destroy relationships, and they are **NOT** the biblical model of navigating conflict in a healthy way!

Read Matthew 18:15-17. This passage provides the most succinct description of the conflict resolution process between individual believers.

1. According to verse 15, who is tasked with initiating the conflict resolution process? The one offended or the one who did the offending?

   a. How many people should be involved at the first step? Why do you think many Christians involve more people than the prescribed amount? The Bible has a name for this.

What is it? (See Proverbs 18:8, 20:19, 26:20, 26:22).

    b. What is the GOAL after step one?

2. If the GOAL is not obtained after the first step, what is the second step found in verse 16?

    a. How many people should be involved at the second step? Again, why do you think many Christians involve more people than the prescribed amount?

    b. Also, once someone engages in the conflict resolution process detailed here, does he or she have the option to stop after step one if the GOAL is not met? (Hint – "Take" is an imperative command, assuming the GOAL is not met).

3. If the GOAL is not obtained after the second step, what is the third step found in verse 17?

a. With the third step, it now moves into a more public sphere because it now involves what entity?

b. Does this mean the offended one stands up and interrupts the service on a Sunday morning to air out his or her offense and call out the offender?

4. Why do you think believers in general struggle in this area of conflict resolution? What are some ways you can be a part of the solution rather than a contributing factor to the problem?

Epidemic #2: Lack of True Community

Introduction: In this section we look at one of the epidemics that is spreading and doing great harm to the Church – a lack of true community. True community is what many believers are starving for. To be in a group that spurs you on to greater fellowship with the Lord and with one another is indeed ideal. However, is that ideal attainable in the Church?

Unfortunately, the Church has been practicing "social distancing" long before it became popular in modern society. For some (I will call them "Lone Wolf Christians") have given up on the community of the local church, citing the failures, hypocrisy, lack of pure vision, and many other supposed shortcomings. For them, it becomes much easier to ***complain***, ***criticize***, and eventually ***ostracize*** themselves from the local church. This heart attitude is exposed through lack of engagement in local church ministry, and it can show up in any the following ways:

1. *Lone Wolf Christians have no value for physical "in presence" church attendance.* To Lone Wolf Christians, it does not matter if they come or not. It could literally be decided by a flip of the coin. They say things like: "I can pick up the sermon online," "Let's not be legalistic about it," "I can have church with my family at home," and "I really am busy." Imagine someone

17

saying the same things about SEC football tickets, amusement park tickets, or a fun day planned with family! It just would not happen. In Hebrews 10:24-25, the author uses the phrase: "Do not forsake." This phrase has the idea of leaving behind, or leaving in a lurch, to desert, or to abandon. It is so vital to understand that the Lord would not have us leave the local church in a lurch or abandon our responsibilities there to be a part of the building project.

2. *The only ministry Lone Wolf Christians are involved in is the one(s) that they are in charge of!* The **ONLY** ministry worth being involved in with the local church, in their mind, is the one they value or control. Although not openly stated, the reason behind this is because they believe they can do it better than anyone else, and many of them do not want to submit themselves to the authority of someone else. Ultimately, it is a rebellious pride issue!

3. *Lone Wolf Christians feel that the local church is optional and does not really "add" anything to their ministry.* These types of Christians see little to no value in the teaching and equipping ministry of their local church. They are typically "getting fed" somewhere other than a local church, and thus they can take or leave gathering on Sundays.

4. *Lone Wolf Christians view their ministry as separate and distinct from the local church.* In other words, if Lone Wolf Christians left a local church, they could continue on with their present ministries without even a hiccup. In fact, for many Lone Wolf Christians, being at their local church is viewed as a time for them to **REST** from their ministry rather than to engage with it.

We have to remember: God has value in the day-to-day engagement with believers in the local church. It is worth considering a question: How can believers consistently engage in the "one anothers" of Scripture if they never see anyone in person? On the flip side: How can others "one another" you if you are never seen?

Another negative outcome of a lack of community in local churches is the increased prevalence of gossip. Gossip is rampant in local churches! For some, it is just easier to be negative and nitpicky, exploring and discussing other's faults and failures rather than being a part of the solution.[1] This is common, and it is what the world does constantly.[2] In as clear of language as possible, we must recognize that gossip is a work of the flesh! Since that is true, and, since the automatic result of sin is **death** (Romans 6:23a), death is the consequence every time someone gossips! (Proverbs 16:28) Additionally, all must understand that even when one just "listens" to gossip, that listener is complicit in the behavior. By doing so, the listener encourages the gossip to continue (Proverbs 26:20). To put it even more bluntly, when the Church engages in gossip, the people involved are destroying the very fellowship that Jesus Christ is attempting to build! They are setting themselves up in direct opposition to Jesus Christ! This type of behavior exposes people and their true agenda in the local church. Thus, it is time to care more about the health of the Church, than tantalizing one's sense by hearing or communicating juicy, sordid details about others.

As a result of the gossip culture in local churches, cliques are very common in the Church. In all fairness, it is natural for many people to be drawn to others who are most like them. If someone shares the same interests, hobbies, personalities, convictions, then it makes sense that they would get along. In fact, it is so common that this is exactly what the world does! However, as natural as this is, the Church does not function on this principle. It functions on the principle of "one anothers" regardless of social background, interests, or hobbies, because believers are all one body in Christ (Galatians 3:26-28). The temptation of homogeneity is huge in the church culture today. People go to churches and hang out with people in those churches who are most like them in how they look, how they talk, how they school their kids, how they worship, etc. Again, although this is natural, this is **NOT** a biblical concept or ideal. In fact, Jesus Christ built His church on the principle of diversity in individual parts for the betterment of the whole (1 Corinthians 12:4-7). Instead of valuing this diversity for the sake of the health of the Church, many believers do everything in their power to keep their own individual groups together, preferring comfort to health.

Thoughtful Quote: "More than at any time in church history, believers and seekers are looking for community. In an age where we are more 'connected' than ever (through social media), we are less connected where it really matters – community."[3]

Read Acts 2:42-47. True community in the Church is going to come when we are occupied with the same things. This passage describes what those things are.

1. According to verse 42, there are two things that the early Church "continued steadfastly" in. What were they?

    a. Why would continuing steadfastly in the apostles' doctrine be important?

    b. Why could continuing steadfastly in fellowship be important?

21

2. The phrase "with one accord" in verse 46 describes unanimity in mind, agenda, and mission. How might this type of unanimity impact true community?

    a. What happens when believers are not "with one accord?" How does that manifest itself in the church?

3. Some Christians have given up on the community of the local church and have become "Lone Wolf Christians." These Christians view attendance in a local church as optional, and they view their ministry as the ONLY one worth being a part of. How does this mentality hurt them and hurt others in the church? (See Hebrews 10:24-25, and Ephesians 4:16).

4. When community is non-existent, gossip is typically rampant. For some, it is just easier to be negative, nitpicky, and to explore other people's faults and failures. Why is this destructive to true community? (See Proverbs 16:28, 26:20).

5. True community struggles to grab hold when cliques are common. For most people, it is natural to be drawn to people who are the most like us. The Church, however, is designed to be a unity built on diversity. How can we be aware of and avoid cliques in our local body?

Epidemic #3: Lost Art of Disciple-Making[1]

Introduction: In this section, we look at another epidemic that is spreading and doing great harm to the Church – the lost the art of disciple-making. The making of disciples is the Church's **primary** function, and yet oftentimes this task does not enter our thinking on a day-to-day basis. Much of what passes for discipleship in churches today is a western model of academia where the church produces "students," NOT future disciple-makers. For some, this message will be a simple reminder to re-focus, and, for others, this will be a paradigm shift in thinking.

Disciple-making is the art of passing on both who and what one is and then empowering disciples to go forth and do the same. To use a non-biblical example, when a carpenter teaches an apprentice, he or she gives the apprentice on-the-job training. The carpenter sets the protégé on the opposite end of a two-by-four and instructs how to measure, cut, and hammer. The apprentice makes mistakes, but, little by little, he learns. The hope is that eventually the apprentice goes on to be independent, though his mentor will be the first one he or she calls when he or she has a question. Similarly, disciple-making is the process of exposing our daily lives to those whom we teach while we eat, drink, cry, and serve together. See Acts 20:36-38 and notice how disciple-making is teaching by life, truth of the Word of God, and example. See also 1 Thessalonians 1:6-8; 2:13-14.

Unfortunately, churches have lost the art of making disciples, and they have replaced disciple-making with the act of making followers, or worse, students. Churches have infused a western way of thinking into the disciple-making model, and they now see disciple-making as sending the best men and women the church has to offer to schools of theology with the hope they will return as capable professionals. Although a lot of information is accumulated in this way, this is not disciple-making. Teaching students is not a substitute for making disciples. A complete overhaul in thinking is in order.

This complete re-vamp in our thinking requires trusting in God's person and in God's method. The Church must be willing to trust God to work through others, and she must learn that making disciple-makers and micromanaging are **<u>NOT</u>** the same. In this sense, biblical disciple-making carries with it risk-taking. Consider that as soon as Paul told Timothy to entrust the teaching to faithful men who would in turn teach it to others, he and Timothy lost their control. This was a good thing, as disciple-making is empowering others to do what the mentor can do and then trusting them to do it.

Let's further consider the art of disciple-making.

Thoughtful Quotes: "Every generation since Christ has witnessed the complete rebirth of the entire church through some form of evangelism. Evangelism, followed by discipleship, is critical for the growth and future of Christ's church. Across the world there exist multitudes of physically "empty" church buildings, empty because they failed in the most fundamental and basic element of Christianity: passing on the truth of God's Word to the next generation."[2]

"The Great Commission is surely one of the most disobeyed commands in all of Scripture!" – Multiple authors.

"The Great Commission is mostly viewed as the Great Suggestion." – Multiple authors.

Read Matthew 28:18-20 and 2 Timothy 2:2.

1. There is one command in the Great Commission passage of Matthew 28:19-20. What is the command? What are the three participles describing how a believer EXECUTES the command?

2. Many Christians and churches talk about discipleship and disciple-making, but very few are engaged in it. Why do you think that is the case? On a personal level, how could you grow in this area?

3. WHO is responsible for making disciples?

a. The Church is supposed to be a disciple-making factory. Why do you suppose the Church, at times, has fallen down in this area throughout history?

4. What is the difference between a "disciple" AND a "disciple-maker?" What are some practical ways we can encourage disciples to become disciple-makers?

5. Biblical disciple-making is the process of exposing our daily lives to those whom we teach while we eat, drink, cry, serve and live together. Why do you think this concept has been replaced with a more western model of student-teacher rather than master-apprentice?

Epidemic #4: Consumeristic Thinking

Introduction: In this section, we look at another epidemic that is spreading and doing great harm to the Church – a consumeristic view of church. The question - "What's in it for me?" is the wrong question to ask when it comes to the Church, and yet, for many, this question permeates their thinking. Much of modern Christian culture views church as one more entity in life that exists to meet one's personal needs. If a church does not do so, many are quick to move on down the road to the next church that will. This mentality is missing the "main point" of what Church should be about. The question is **NOT**, "What's in it for me?" but rather, "What's my part in what Jesus Christ wants to do?"

Unfortunately, people choose churches that "fit them" and meet their checklist of preferences, just as one would choose a car or a new pair of jeans. If the other church down the road offers a more pleasant experience, they will move their business there. For many churches, this puts pressure on them to be gimmicky and trendy to solve the issue. This mentality completely misses the point! Church is a place where members of a body come together for purposes beyond themselves! It is an invitation to join Christ in what He is already doing in the world, not an invitation for Christ to affirm our self-actualization! Consumption has NEVER been the goal of true discipleship! Christianity has fallen into the trap of "spectator-itis!"

Many believers want to self-direct their own spiritual journey without any value or consideration given to God's method via local churches. Christians want every other Bible teacher except the one they already have because the guy from "over yonder hill" is definitely more spiritual and has a higher I.Q. than the pastor or elders. In fact, many believers decide for themselves what Bible study program they are going to be involved with and what ministry they are going to do, and they never once stop to consider the mechanism (i.e., Ephesians 4:11-16) that God has clearly put into place for the benefit of their spiritual lives. Self-diagnosis and self-treatment are en vogue due to the advent of Google and the amount of information readily available at a click of a mouse or the touch of a screen. Culturally, people can self-diagnose their own medical issues, their own home repairs, their own car problems, their own personality issues, etc.!

If believers are content with the doctrinal position of their local church, why would they search the internet for additional Bible teaching where they might be unsure of: (1) Where the Bible teacher is truly at doctrinally? AND (2) What the Bible teacher's character truly is? Some of the Bible teachers on the internet may not even *qualify* to be an elder per 1 Timothy 3:1-7, and yet they are preferred to the local men in the body just because the online teachers can give a good speech!

The Bible describes the value of assembling with other believers in a context where there are appointed elders, deacons, gifted pastor-teachers, and fellow believers all exercising their spiritual gifts, "agitating" one another towards love and good deeds, correcting/rebuking/exhorting one another, etc. These things cannot happen in isolation! So, what is *God's* mechanism for accomplishing *His* mission?

Thoughtful Quotes: "The concept of consumerism has completely infiltrated the church. People go to Sunday services 'to get something,' and, if they don't 'get it,' they move on to the next church and they continue shopping. Church is a place where members of a body come together for purposes beyond themselves! It is an invitation to join Christ in what He is already doing in the world, not an invitation for Christ to affirm our self-actualization."[1]

"The church needs to stop with the gimmicks. She can end her trinket peddling. She can cool it with the Star Wars sermon series. She simply needs to believe and preach the Word of God!"[2]

Churches are too little like training centers to shape up the saints and too much like cardiopulmonary wards at the local hospital. We have proliferated self-indulgent consumer religion, the what-can-the-church-do-for-me-syndrome. We are too easily satisfied with conventional success:

bodies, bucks, and buildings.[3]

The church has become like a college football game…"there are 22 people on the field in desperate need of rest and there are 40,000 people in the stands in desperate need of exercise."[4] – spoken by Bud Wilkinson, head football of the University of Oklahoma in 1963.

Read Ephesians 4:7-16. This is God's mechanism for equipping the saints for accomplishing the team goal (i.e. disciple-making).

1. Christianity has fallen into the trap of "spectator-itis" - a group of people coming together as spectators who watch other people DO the ministry. Why do you think that is?

2. God clearly has a different plan for the Church gathering, and He put two types of tools in place according to Ephesians 4:7-11. What are those two parts or tools that God gave?

3. According to verse 12, why were the two parts or tools from verses 7-11 given?

   a. So, WHO is in the ministry according to verse 12? WHO benefits when this entity is engaged in the ministry?

b. In putting together Ephesians 4:7-16 and Ephesians 2:10, how does this whole process fit together?

4. Why is coming to the unity of THE faith AND the unity of the knowledge of the Son of God so important?

5. What is the potential NEGATIVE outcome of not taking advantage of this mechanism in the local church? (See verse 14).

Epidemic #5: Lack of Personal Intimacy with God

Introduction: In this section, we look at another epidemic that is spreading and doing great harm to the Church – a lack of personal intimacy with God. Many Christians spend more time covering up their sins or weaknesses by pretending to be someone they are not. Rather than frankly admitting their weaknesses and attempting to take advantage of God's resources in Christ, many Christians are content with living an incongruent public and private life. "Fake it till you make it" may be a popular sales slogan, but it has NO place in Christianity.

The conscience is defined as one's own witness, and it denotes an abiding consciousness, which bears inner witness to one's own moral conduct. It is the self-awareness of distinguishing between right and wrong. In the grand scheme of things, the "conscience" is a built-in mechanism whereby people are given immediate internal feedback as to whether or not what they are doing, thinking, or feeling is right or wrong. As such, it helps believers specifically understand what SOURCE they are living their life from (i.e. either the flesh/sin nature or the Spirit of God).

As believers, the conscience is designed as a tool to spring them into action. When recognizing they are out of fellowship with the Lord, they are able to immediately confess their sins, so their fellowship with the

Lord might be restored. When this happens, the conscience is used as a tool to fulfill God's purpose in the believer's life. It is clear from the Scriptures that fellowship with the Lord and abiding in Christ are the keys to living a fruitful and productive Christian life. However, too often this does not happen, and believers ignore their consciences, which then takes them down a very dangerous path - a path where many believers are content with living life out of fellowship with the Lord, becoming increasingly more "O.K." with ignoring their conscience and thus spending more time walking according to the flesh.

There are a few reasons why this has become such a pandemic in our churches:

1. *Christian culture allows for prideful self-satisfaction* – If one is honest with themselves, many Christians give lip-service to wanting to do and be everything that God wants them to do and be. However, when it comes down to it, Christians often do whatever they want to do and then try to justify it before others and God. Ultimately, believers are more content to be out of fellowship with God if that means they get to do what they want to do. The implications of that statement are mind-blowing! These believers are basically saying they would rather walk according to the flesh and take all of the consequences that comes with that approach. Can anyone articulate even ONE benefit of walking according to the flesh? The

clear biblical answer is NO, NOT ONE! In a sense, believers are saying to themselves, "Abundant life? I think my life is pretty good as it is! I'll just take the life I have (i.e., I will settle for much less) if I get to make my own decisions without any course correction by God or anyone else!"

2. *Correction is a true friend* - It is O.K. to be wrong and to receive correction! This is one of God's tools to grow believers spiritually. If this is true, then why do believers fight this so intensely? Is it because believers are stupid? (See Proverbs 12:1) Interestingly enough, some of the specifically stated **negative** purposes of the teaching of the Word of God are: Reproof, Correction, and Instruction (i.e., meaning child discipline). (See 2 Timothy 3:16-17). Why would God use those negative purposes for His Word? Verse 17 of 2 Timothy 3 tells us it is so that the man of God may be "complete" or mature, so that he might be thoroughly equipped for good works.

3. *Authority structures are the believer's friend* - God has placed different authority structures in the lives of Christians for their safety, for their good, and for their spiritual growth. Some of those authority structures include: government, employers, church leaders, teachers, parents, etc. It is unfortunate, yet true, that many Christians have learned, trained themselves, and tolerated rebellion in most, **if not all**, of these authority areas at some point in their

lives. What each one must understand is that this is **NOT** good for one's spiritual growth, and it is very unprofitable for believers who engage in this type of behavior! (1 Peter 5:5-7, Hebrews 13:17)

The need for personal intimacy and fellowship with God needs to be examined and considered as paramount in importance for the Church.

Thoughtful Quote: "We live in a society that is not sorry it did something wrong, but merely sorry it got caught doing something wrong!"[1]

Some interesting statistics to consider:

1. Barna Research surveyed 718 self-identified Christians from a variety of denominations to find what extent their actions and attitudes line up with Jesus's. Researchers found only 1 in 7 Christians manage to hold Christ-like beliefs and also act in Christ-like ways.[2]

2. 74% of married men and 68% of married women said in an anonymous survey that they would cheat on their spouse if they knew they would never get caught.[3]

Read 1 Timothy 1:18-20. God utilizes the conscience for believers' own good and to encourage personal intimacy with Him by allowing believers to realize when they have done something to knock themselves out of fellowship with the Lord.

1. When our conscience is pricked, and we realize that what we are

doing, thinking, or feeling is wrong (i.e. sinful), what should we do about it immediately? (See 1 John 1:9).

2. According to 1 Timothy 1:18-19, it is imperative for the believer to "fight" or "wage the good warfare" by holding tight of what two things?

    a. Why do you think it is important to hold tight to THE faith?

    b. Why do you think it is important to hold tight to a GOOD conscience?

3. What happened to the two men Paul mentions in verse 19 who had rejected both "the faith" and a "good conscience?"

a. What does it mean to be shipwrecked?

b. What stood out to you about the other two "bad" examples given in the lives of King David (2 Samuel 11-12, Psalm 51) and King Saul (1 Samuel 15)?

4. Why do you think many people struggle to receive correction well? Why do you think many people struggle to value different authority structures in their lives? How do these two things relate to our personal intimacy and fellowship with the Lord?

ENDNOTES

Introduction:

1. For a supplemental support resource see Grace Community Fellowship's YouTube channel (https://www.youtube.com/channel/UCk0ddf5eD5SASveZJHwKaEQ) and select the Epidemics of Christianity playlist. This study booklet was developed from those series of messages.

What Is Jesus Up To?:

1. Lynn Smith, "Church's Success Built on Blend of Yuppies, Marketing," Los Angeles Times, accessed July 1, 2020, last modified August 20, 1989, https://www.latimes.com/archives/la-xpm-1989-08-20-mn-1447-story.html.
2. J. Hampton Keathley III, ABC's For Christian Growth, (Richardson, TX: Biblical Studies Press, 1996), 345.

Epidemic #1: Poor Conflict Resolution:

1. Kenneth Boa, "Conflict Management," Bible.org, accessed July 1, 2020, https://bible.org/seriespage/conflict-management.
2. Ken Sande, The Peacemaker, (Grand Rapids: Baker Publishing Group, 2004), 29.
3. Jean Varnier, Community and Growth, (New York: Paulist Press, 1989), 120-121.
4. Alexander Strauch, If you Bite & Devour One Another: Biblical Principles for Handling Conflict, (Littleton, CO.: Lewis and Roth Publishers, 2011), 18.
5. Larry Crabb, The Safest Place on Earth, (Nashville: Word Publishing, 1999), 40.

Epidemic #2: Lack of True Community:

1. Many Christians, starting with me, master the art of pointing out the bad from a young age. For much of my Christian journey, I thought it was my job to find the errors in everything from sermons to the lives of those around me. I was like a stealth ninja.

My only job was to make sure every mistake was pointed out. And after finding the errors, my friends and I would gather for a time of 'reflection.'...Here's the problem with cynicism: as long as it's your default perspective, you can't be a catalyst for change. Not for the good, at least. And I say 'perspective' because cynicism is all about how you see things. You and I can look at the same person, situation, etc. and see two different things. The only difference is the filter through which we see it. – Frank Powell, "10 Toxic Christians in the Church Today," FaithIt, accessed July 1, 2020, last modified June 11, 2019, https://faithit.com/10-toxic-christians-in-the-church-today-frank-powell/.

2. So often, people seek out church because they need a reprieve, a refuge from the emotional drama of day to day living. However, far too often church relationships find a way to add to your drama. Now, I get that we're all imperfect and that any group will have their own conflict, but some churches seem to do drama more than others. Our jobs, family dynamics and friendships provides us with enough opportunity to be gossiped about, back-stabbed, and pushed to the margins – we don't need to add to that. – Benjamin L. Corey, "10 Reasons Why People Leave Church," Formerly Fundie, accessed July 1, 2020, https://www.benjaminlcorey.com/10-reasons-why-people-leave-church/.

3. Author's personal notes.

Epidemic #3: Lost Art of Disciple-Making:

1. This chapter leans heavily on the DM2 (Disciple Makers Multiplied) Manual entitled "Making Disciple-Makers" (www.dm2usa.org).

2. Bret Nazworth, "Making Disciple-Makers," DM2 (Disciple Makers Multiplied), www.dm2usa.org.

Epidemic #4: Consumeristic Thinking:

1. Brett McCracken, "21 Challenges Facing the 21st Century Church," Brett McCracken, accessed July 1, 2020, last modified October 27, 2016, https://www.brettmccracken.com/blog/blog/2016/10/27/21-challenges-facing-the-21st-century-church.

2. Unknown Author, "What's Wrong With Church?," Off the Page,

accessed July 8, 2018, https://offthepage.com/2016/02/17/whats-wrong-with-church/.

3. Bill Hull, The Disciple-Making Pastor: Leading Others on the Journey of Faith, (Grand Rapids: Baker Publishing Group, 2007), 18.

4. Barry Popik, "Entry from June 22, 2014," The Big Apple, accessed July 1, 2020, https://www.barrypopik.com/index.php/new_york_city/entry/football_is_22_people_on_the_field.

Epidemic #5: Lack of Personal Intimacy with God:

1. Author's personal notes.

2. George Barna, "Christians: More Like Jesus or Pharisees?," Barna, accessed July 1, 2020, last modified June 3, 2013, https://www.barna.com/research/christians-more-like-jesus-or-pharisees/.

3. Author Unknown, "These Cheating Statistics Probably Hit Close to Home (Statistically)," Newswire, accessed July 1, 2020, last modified April 22, 2014, https://www.newswire.com/these-cheating-statistics-probably/271424

ABOUT THE AUTHOR

Dr. John Thomas Clark holds his bachelor's degree in Mathematics from the University of Texas at San Antonio, has a master's degree in Theology (Th.M.) from Tyndale Theological Seminary and Biblical Institute, and a doctorate degree (DMin) with an emphasis on expository preaching from Dallas Theological Seminary. He values systematic, verse-by-verse Bible teaching and enjoys drawing out truths from the original languages.

John has served as the Senior Pastor of Grace Community Fellowship in Newnan, Georgia since September 2016. Additionally, John is a founding board member of DM2 (Disciple Makers Multiplied), a mission organization focused on pastoral training and discipleship of other disciple-makers. John leads DM2's field to Liberia, Africa and travels there twice a year to train pastors. John's first and foremost ministry lies in being a husband to his wife, Carrie, and a loving father to their five children. For more teaching from Pastor John Clark, please visit www.gracenewnan.org.

Made in the USA
Columbia, SC
13 September 2020

20215928R00031